W9-AMB-414

THE BLESSED SACRAMENT
GOD WITH US

"Behold I am with you all days, even to the consummation of the world."
—Matthew 28:20

THE BLESSED SACRAMENT
GOD WITH US

"My delights were to be with the children of men."
—Proverbs 8:30

TAN Books
An Imprint of Saint Benedict Press, LLC
Charlotte, North Carolina

Nihil Obstat: ☩ Stephen Schappler, O.S.B.
              Abbot Coadjutor
              Immaculate Conception Province

Imprimatur: ☩ Charles Hubert Le Blond
             Bishop of St. Joseph

Originally published by the Benedictine Convent of Perpetual Adoration, Clyde, Missouri, under the title *God with Us—In the Blessed Sacrament*. (2nd edition, 1942, 58,000 copies).

Retypeset and republished in 2000 by TAN Books, an Imprint of Saint Benedict Press, LLC.

Library of Congress Control No.: 00-131564

ISBN: 978-0-89555-661-5

Printed and bound in the United States of America.

TAN Books
An Imprint of Saint Benedict Press, LLC
Charlotte, North Carolina

2010

Our Hidden God

O Godhead hid, devoutly I adore Thee,
Who truly art within the forms before me,
To Thee my heart I bow with bended knee
As failing quite in contemplating Thee.

ST. THOMAS AQUINAS

CONTENTS

THE BLESSED
SACRAMENT
GOD WITH US

"The Lord is there."
—Ezechiel 48:35

Chapter 1

Our Emmanuel

THE thirty-three years of His earthly life seemed all too short to our Divine Saviour, whose "delights were to be with the children of men." (*Prov.* 8:31). To be born for us, to live a toilsome life and to suffer and sacrifice Himself for us by a most painful death did not exhaust the love of the Incarnate Son of God. He wished to **remain** among us even after His ascension into Heaven and, by a perpetual miracle, to continue in a mystical manner the mysteries of His earthly life and of His sacred Passion and death. This He accomplished by instituting the Most Blessed Sacrament. Oh, wondrous love, which compels the Son of God to remain continually with us on our altars! Truly, the mercy of our Redeemer has reached even to the depths of Divine love in order to give us this adorable Sacrament.

1

The infinite **omnipotence** of God could present us with nothing greater; His infinite **wisdom** knew of nothing better; His infinite **love** could bestow on us nothing more holy than the adorable Sacrament of the Altar. Let us admire and adore the amazing abasement of the Lord of the universe, the Son of the Most High, in so humbling Himself for our salvation as to conceal Himself under the lowly species of bread.

A Heavenly Manna

The Most Blessed Sacrament was prefigured by the manna in the desert, for this heavenly food is similar to the manna in its properties and in its name. When the Israelites saw the bread which had miraculously fallen from Heaven, they exclaimed: *"Manhu! . . .* What is this!" (*Exod.* 16:15). And thereafter the mysterious food was called **manna.**

How admirably is the name "Heavenly Manna" suited to the great mystery of the altar! For this Divine Mystery contains so much that is wonderful that we cannot devoutly reflect upon It without exclaiming in utter astonishment: **What is this!** Infinite

Majesty, which the heavens cannot contain, encloses Itself in a tiny Host! The King of Glory deigns to dwell upon earth and to deliver Himself into the hands of sinners! The Second Person of the Blessed Trinity, who is of the same essence with the Father and the Holy Spirit, deigns to make Himself the food of man!

What food is this that imparts so much strength to the heart, inflames the will with so burning a fire, enlightens the understanding with so brilliant a light and imparts such purity to the soul! What a heavenly banquet is here spread before us! What goodness, what love! Without doubt, this is **the greatest gift** God has deigned to bestow upon us; it is the most magnificent work of His goodness, the clearest proof and the most manifest testimony of His love.

Let us, therefore, hasten to the Most Blessed Sacrament; let us hasten to our God ever abiding in our midst on the altar. There we will supplicate for graces, there make atonement for the countless sins and crimes committed against Him, there praise His goodness, there glorify Him. This is our great and holy vocation as Catholics. **Our God is there present** under the appearance of bread; He is there **really and substantially.** Him whom we hope once to behold in glory, face to face, we now behold in His silent, mysterious majesty and tranquility. He is enthroned in His Tabernacle, in the midst of the Church Militant. He looks upon us as we struggle and suffer; He is ever at our side to aid and refresh us in all our tribulations. He helps us to fight and conquer the world with its temptations, its vanities and its miseries; and when, weary from the strife, we at length depart from this life, He will raise us up to His Heavenly Father and will give us the crown of victory.

What fathomless depths of the riches of God's mercy are made manifest to us in the Most Blessed Sacrament! Come, come, therefore, kneel down and glorify in fervent prayers and sacred hymns of praise, thanksgiving and jubilation, our **Emmanuel,** our **God with us.**

Chapter 2

The Mystery of Love

WE are children of the Heavenly Father. No father has ever loved his children as much as our Father in Heaven loves us. To prove His love, He gave us a gift so great and so sublime that He could not have given a greater: He gave us His only-begotten Son. And the only-begotten Son of the Father loved us so much that He not only sacrificed Himself for us on the Cross, but gave Himself to us wholly and for all times in the Most Blessed Sacrament of the Altar.

God is love, and the entire strength of Divine love reveals itself in this mystery of love. Even the Angels of Heaven could never have thought that a God could so love men as to give Himself to them as their food, to enter into their hearts in order to enkindle in them a return of love. Who can doubt the love of God when he contemplates the Sacred Host? Is it not a perfect expression of the greatness of the love of God for the children of men? There, from the Tabernacle, He addresses to us those words of infinite love and invincible patience: "Come to me, all you that labour and are burdened, and I will refresh you." (*Matt.* 11:28).

In no other Sacrament does our Divine Lord show the excess of His love in so touching and wonderful a manner as in the Most Holy Eucharist. From the other Sacraments, too, flow countless and invaluable graces, all of which betoken God's immeasurable love for men; but the adorable Sacrament of the Altar contains the **source** of all graces, the **treasury** of Divine riches, yes, **Eternal Love Itself.** "God is love," says St. John, and this God of love, Jesus Christ, Our Lord, is really and substantially present in the Blessed Sacrament.

The Saints cherished the adorable Sacrament of the Altar as the Sacrament of Love. St. Thomas Aquinas, the Angelic Doctor, called It the "Sacrament of Love, the pledge of love." St. Bernard, all aglow with fervor, cried out, "It was love that urged Him to dwell in the Blessed Sacrament; love invented It, love gave It, love replenishes It with the riches of His love. Verily, there we may read the Love of all love!" St. Philip Neri, when dying, seeing the priest bringing the Holy Viaticum, exclaimed: "O my Love! Give me my Love!"

Animated with a like faith, and inflamed with the love of these Saints, let us approach the Sacred Host and look deeply into the Fount of Love. Let us meditate upon Its greatness and Its depth, that our cold hearts may be warmed by the wonderful force of Its attraction.

A Threefold Gift of Love

We cannot sufficiently prize the Most Blessed Sacrament. It is the heart of the Church, the center of our holy Religion, the well-spring of our Faith. The Holy Eucharist is our Sovereign Good, the most precious treasure we possess here on earth. In the Sacrament of the Altar, we behold three great manifestations of our Saviour's love:

1. Jesus offers Himself as a Victim of sacrifice for us in the Holy Eucharist. Daily He renews on our altars in an unbloody manner His bloody sacrifice of Calvary. As on the Cross He offered to the Eternal Father

His Body, His Blood, His Heart, so in every Holy Mass He offers Himself anew, entirely and unreservedly.

Holy Mass is the most worthy sacrifice of **praise** that can be offered to God. The praise and adoration which is given to God by all men, angels and saints cannot be compared with the glory that is given Him by **one Holy Mass.** For there His only-begotten Son, who is one with Him in essence, equal to Him in all things, "the unspotted mirror of God's majesty" (*Wis.* 7:26), offers Himself to Him.

The Sacrifice of the Mass is likewise the most sublime sacrifice of **thanksgiving,** infinitely more pleasing to God than all the sacrifices of thanksgiving which the Old Law in the course of centuries had offered to Him; it is the most effectual sacrifice of **supplication,** because in the Sacrifice of the Mass the Son of God Himself is our Mediator with the Heavenly Father; and finally, it is the most efficacious sacrifice of **atonement** that can be offered for the living and the dead, for in Holy Mass the Precious Blood of Christ is shed anew in a mystical manner. Numberless sinners have obtained the grace of true conversion and perseverance through the Holy Sacrifice of the Mass. Daily a rich stream of graces flows from the altar into Purgatory to alleviate the sufferings of the Poor Souls and to make satisfaction for their sins.

2. Jesus offers Himself to us as our Food in Holy Communion. He desires to be for us the manna that nourishes and strengthens us on our pilgrimage to the land of promise, to our heavenly home. In Holy Communion He gives us **light** to dispel the darkness of our spirit; He gives us **consolation** to support us in sufferings; **peace** and **rest** to pacify our heart; **courage** to make us strong in our trials and temptations. What incomprehensible love on the part of Jesus! What inestimable happiness for us poor, weak creatures of earth.

And oh, how wonderful! In a thousand Hosts He is as in one; His Presence is in each place where there is a consecrated Host, and each communicant receives Him whole and entire, though a hundred thousand should receive Him. Hundreds of thousands receive Him and He rests in hundreds of thousands of places at the same time. Such a miracle only an omnipotent God can accomplish.

3. Jesus dwells continually in our midst in the Blessed Sacrament. Day and night He abides among us under the lowly species of bread, in the narrow Tabernacles of our churches. Here He is not only our infinitely great God, but also our merciful Saviour and our most faithful friend. The same miracles He wrought for the corporally sick during His earthly life, He performs in our days from the Tabernacle for those spiritually ill. He gives sight to the **"blind"** by granting them light to see the evil of sin, the value of things eternal, the value of Crosses and sufferings, the value of resignation to the will of God. He gives power of movement to the **"lame"** by prompting their sluggish will to resolve and act for His love alone. He raises the **"dead"** to life by calling souls from the death of sin to the life of grace.

For every spiritual ailment His love holds a remedy in readiness. Are you **abandoned and sorrowful?** On the altar you will find the heavenly Comforter. Are you **poor in virtue?** In the Tabernacle He who is infinitely rich is waiting to share His treasures with you. Are you **troubled on account of your sins,** and do you sigh for pardon? Go to the altar! Jesus, the all-merciful God, will receive you with open arms. He will help you to do everything necessary for true repentance. With His own Heart's Blood He will purify your soul and impart to you a strength which will sustain you until you have reached the "Mountain of God," the celestial paradise.

In your temporal needs and your physical ailments, Jesus in the Tabernacle will also be your Friend, your Father and your Physician. Countless is the number of those who, burdened with anxiety and care, have found help and relief before the Tabernacle. Many, too, are the bodily cures wrought through the Blessed Sacrament. At the shrine of Our Lady of Lourdes, where countless miracles are wrought each year, it is usually at the time the sick are blessed with the Most Blessed Sacrament that the miraculous cures are effected.

God's Greatest Gift of Love

In the Blessed Sacrament we possess, indeed, God's greatest gift of love. We measure the love of the giver by the greatness and costliness of his gift, by the advantages and benefits derived therefrom. Who, then, can fathom the love of our Saviour in bestowing upon us the inestimable three-fold gift of the Holy Eucharist?

Jesus is present in the Blessed Sacrament with His Divinity and Humanity, His Soul and Body, His Flesh and Blood. Through His Real Presence, the Tabernacle becomes the treasury of all riches, for it contains Jesus, the fountain of all grace, with the infinite plenitude of His Divine treasures. There He holds them ever in readiness for us; He calls and invites us to come and take them. His presence is the life of the Church, the life, the joy and delight of every loving soul.

Jesus Is Present in His Divinity

Our Lord and Saviour, present in the Tabernacle, veils His Divinity, His majesty and splendor beneath the robe of humility and abasement. By the garb of lowliness He conceals all His Divine attributes and perfections. As we gaze on the Sacred Host, our bodily eye beholds only the appearance of bread; but the spiritual eye of faith penetrates the veil and beholds the King of kings in His infinite majesty, yet full of mercy, condescension and love.

Oh, how consoling for every faithful soul is the thought: **My Lord and God is here present,** present for love of **me!** With the spouse in the Canticle she can exclaim: "My beloved to me, and I to him!" (*Cant.* 2:16). God is ours; He has given Himself to us poor sinful creatures! Who can comprehend this excess of love? Who can fathom the boundless love that bestows such a priceless gift on poor creatures?

Jesus is ours in His Divinity which has united Itself with His human nature in one Person, and in this union He is present in the Holy Eucharist. Jesus is present with all the merits He acquired by His life, Passion and death, and which derive their infinite value from His Divinity. He is ours with all His Divine attributes and perfections. How this knowledge must console and encourage every faint-hearted, despondent soul!

Here God is most generous, ready to hear and grant our petitions and to impart to us His superabundant graces. Here is God, the all-knowing and all-wise, who sees what is most profitable and necessary for us. Here is God, most faithful and true, who will keep the promise He has made: He will open when we knock, provided our request is not injurious to our soul. Here is God, whose "tender mercies are over all His works" (*Ps.* 144:9), waiting to receive repentant sinners with kindness and love. Here is God, Eternal Love, who wills only what is best for us for time and eternity.

Jesus Is Present in His Humanity

In the adorable Sacrament, Jesus is present in His humanity, with His true **human soul** and His true **human body**. He is present with His true human soul, His noble, holy soul. He is present with that soul which on the Cross endured the unspeakable anguish of being forsaken by His Father. He is present with that soul which perceives as we perceive and feels as we feel—truly and humanly—for He is like unto us in all things, sin excepted. He is present with that soul which, like all human souls, is endowed with the faculties of understanding and free will, which He exercises always in perfect conformity with the will of His Heavenly Father. He is present with His glorified human soul, radiant with infinite beauty and splendor, now incapable of sorrow or suffering. And He loves you, O child of Adam, He loves you unspeakably, not only with His Divine Heart but also with His human soul. He shares with you the treasures of immeasurable merits, of graces and gifts, with which the Triune God has endowed and embellished His most beautiful soul.

In the Blessed Sacrament Jesus is present with His true human body, in which dwells the fullness of Divinity. His Sacred Humanity is now resplendent with heavenly glory and free from all suffering. Yes, Jesus is here present with the same body which He assumed from Mary, the Immaculate Virgin, with the same body in which He endured heat and cold, hunger and thirst, hardships and fatigue, and which He finally sacrificed amidst nameless woe upon the Cross.

Behold, here are the same loving **eyes** that looked upon men with mercy and compassion! Now their tender, fatherly gaze rests upon you as you kneel before the Tabernacle. Here are those **lips** which once spoke such sweet, entrancing words. Now they speak to your heart, but their soft, mysterious whisper is heard only by the ears of your soul.

Here are the same **hands** that once blessed the sick, the afflicted, the repentant sinners and the little children, the blessed hands which wrought so much good. Now He extends them to you, to draw you to His loving Heart, to bless you and to enrich you with His graces.

Here are the sacred **feet** that wearied and fatigued themselves in search of souls; the feet, that, bruised and bleeding, climbed Calvary's heights, and were pierced on the Cross for the salvation of men. From the Tabernacle they invite you to follow in the footsteps of your Divine Saviour and to keep far from the pathways of sin.

Here is present that **Sacred Heart** which beat for sinners in unspeakable love until It broke upon the Cross. In the Sacred Host this amiable Heart still beats for you and for each human soul as warmly and tenderly as It once beat upon the Cross.

Here is present the **Precious Blood** which coursed through every member of the sacred Body of Jesus and which, in love, He shed to the last drop for the world's Redemption. Now It is your nourishment in Holy Communion, and It daily flows in a mystical manner upon the altar to wash away your sins and to adorn your soul with heavenly graces.

The Supreme Judge

But He who dwells in the Most Holy Sacrament is also the awful Judge of the living and the dead. How mild, how silent and patient is the Sacred Host, and yet It is the God of rigorous justice who forges everlasting chains. Under this appearance of bread rests the God-Man, whom the Father has appointed the supreme Judge of mankind: "And He hath given him power to do judgment, because he is the Son of Man." (*John* 5:27). How the sin-laden children of men will lament when this awful Judge comes to pass sentence on them! He has already pronounced judgment upon those who do not receive Him, or who receive Him **unworthily** in Holy Communion, for He has said: "Amen, amen, I say to you: except you eat the flesh of the son of man, and drink his blood, you shall not have life in you." (*John* 6:54). "Whosoever shall eat this bread, or drink the chalice of the Lord unworthily, shall be guilty of the body and of the blood of the Lord." . . . For he that eateth and drinketh unworthily, eateth and drinketh judgment to himself, not discerning the body of the Lord." (*1 Cor.* 11:27, 29).*

---

*It must be noted that this "judgment" is not, in this life, a *final* judgment, for the sin of receiving Holy Communion unworthily (i.e., in the state of mortal sin) will be forgiven like any other sin when confessed with true repentance in the Sacrament of Penance. —*Publisher,* 2000

Chapter 3

Proofs of Love

JESUS CHRIST came into this world to reveal God's love for men and to re-establish the reign of Divine love upon earth. It was an inconceivably great love that caused Him to become man; and during His whole life our Saviour never ceased to give proofs of this love. But at the end of His life He gathered up this Divine love into one grand act, into one great gift of grace, the **Most Holy Eucharist.** Let us, for a moment, contemplate the many splendid testimonials of His love which are manifested in His earthly life, that we may the better comprehend His great love in the Holy Eucharist.

1. The Incarnation

Through the sin of our first parents, mankind had been plunged into the deepest misery. The gates of Heaven were closed, and the children of Adam would have been doomed to eternal perdition had not God taken pity on them. But Divine Mercy, moved with compassion, sent them a Redeemer—a Redeemer who was none other than the Son of God Himself. At the time appointed by the Divine decrees, one of the highest princes of Heaven, the Archangel Gabriel, was sent to the humble Virgin of Nazareth to announce to her that she was chosen to be the Mother of God. Mary spoke her *Fiat,* "Be it done to me according to thy word," and the incomprehensible mystery of the Incarnation was accomplished. In this mystery the Second Person of the most Blessed Trinity united in one Divine Person the human nature and the Divine, thus exalting our nature to the throne of Divinity. What an honor! All this He did for **love** of us, to reconcile us with our offended God, to make us again the children of God. And after His Incarnation, as God-Man, He loved us not only with a Divine love, but also with a truly **human** love.

2. Life and Labors

The thirty years of His hidden life—those years of profound solitude, of abject poverty, of amazing subjection, of laborious work, of deep humility—are they not also a powerful sermon of His **love** for us? For whom did He live this humble, sacrificial life? He lived it for you and for me. And during the three years of His public ministry, the gentle words, the grace-giving doctrines that fell from His lips breathed naught but love. All His prayers, His toils and sufferings loudly proclaimed His love for us. The miracles He wrought sprang from compassion for the children of Adam, from love for the salvation and welfare of souls. Truly did He say, "The Son of Man is come to seek and to save that which was lost." (*Luke* 19:10).

3. Passion and Death

In the sufferings of Jesus there was manifested a wonderful **excess** of love. Great was the love that caused Him to desire to forgive mankind. Greater still was the love that caused Him to desire to drink the bitter chalice of suffering and ignominy which our sins prepared for Him. But it was an **excess of love** that urged Him to lay down His life even for those who He knew would repay His love with coldness and ingratitude.

The Beloved Disciple says: "In this we have known the charity of God because He hath laid down His life for us." (*1 John* 3:16). Yes, from the Cross He preached the most eloquent sermon of love. The drops of Precious Blood flowing from His Wounds, were they not speaking witnesses to His infinite love? His Divine heart opened for us on the Cross, His pierced hands and feet—did they not loudly proclaim His love for sinners? Verily He has lavished so much love upon us that He can truly say: "What is there that I ought to do more to My vineyard, that I have not done to it?" (*Is.* 5:4).

And yet, all these wonderful proofs of love did not satisfy the love of our Saviour. Though He Himself says, "Greater love than this no man hath that a man lay down his life for his friends" (*John* 15:13), His own love could and did go further, because He was not only man but also **God.** Hence He devised a means which would unite and embody all the love already shown us, something that would even surpass and excel all

He had hitherto bestowed, the greatest memorial of His love, the **Holy Eucharist.**

4. The Holy Eucharist

Yes, the Holy Eucharist is, indeed, the greatest proof of Jesus' love for us. With It He gave **Himself**, His whole life, His Passion and death, His Resurrection, His Ascension and glory, His full and unreserved love.

"It would seem," to use the words of Father Faber, "as though He could not separate Himself from Bethlehem and Egypt, from Nazareth and Jerusalem, from Genesareth and Bethania, from Gethsemane and Calvary. It would seem as though He could not abandon a single mystery of the three and thirty years, and therefore, by means of His human nature and His almighty power, would unite and renew them all. **This union and renewal is the Blessed Sacrament** . . . As He then lived upon earth, so now He lives in our midst, but transfigured and veiled to the bodily eyes. As He then offered Himself a sacrifice upon the Cross, so He continues to offer Himself in every Holy Mass for us, only the way and manner of offering is different. Even more: in this

Mystery He becomes our Food as the pledge of our eternal salvation."

Praise and thanksgiving be without end
to the Most Blessed Sacrament!

Chapter 4

Characteristics of the Love of Our Lord in the Eucharist

Benignity

ONE of the most striking marks of true love is **benignity.** Love gives **cheerfully.** Will not a fond mother, a solicitous father, give to a beloved child everything within a parent's power? Jesus Christ in the Blessed Sacrament also gives to His children—and what does He give? "Everything that He has," says St. Augustine; "His grace, His merits, His glory." "He keeps nothing back," says St. Thomas. "He places all the riches of His love into the sacramental gift. In this gift He presents to us all the love of His Incarnation, all the merits of His life and His works, the entire price of Redemption."

Yes, He does still more. He gives us His Person, His Blood, His Life, His Soul,

His Divinity. He becomes the property of man, his possession, his nourishment. What unheard of benignity!

Simplicity

The perfection of love is recognized also in the **manner of giving.** Whosoever gives in a cold, haughty manner causes the needy one to feel his dependence and abjection. Pure love allows only the gift to appear and conceals the hand which gives—yes, conceals even the gift itself in order to rejoice the friend and to turn attention from self. Jesus gives us the Holy Eucharist by the hands of the priest, who is not free from human frailty and even has full liberty of sinning.

In the Eucharist, Jesus conceals His glory, His majesty, His power, and even His sanctity. He likewise veils His Body, His whole Divine Person, so that we may not fear to approach Him.

When God created the first man, He took a little earth and animated it by breathing into it a soul. Jesus Christ, the Son of God, the Son of Man, who in the Eucharist wishes to be our sacrifice, our nourishment and our guest, takes bread, changes it into Himself, and becomes living Bread. How simple is His sacramental state! Kings appear in the splendor of their royal majesty, often with great pomp and at great expense to their subjects, for they must be received in a manner becoming to their rank. Jesus Christ, on the contrary, becomes a burden to no one; His palace is a Tabernacle, His residence a ciborium, His resting place a corporal. In His Eucharistic state He requires little room. He is unassuming and very simple, and rich and poor alike may approach Him without fear and without formality.

Fidelity

Another characteristic mark of love is **fidelity,** or faithfulness. In the Holy Eucharist Jesus displays the most remarkable fidelity, for He remains with us perpetually and is always at our disposal. Day and night He waits for us without growing weary or impatient. His love never wavers, never forsakes us. Though all the world should turn against us, though all our friends should forsake us, Jesus in the

Blessed Sacrament remains ever true. His love perseveres even when He is abandoned, despised, blasphemed. Truly, His love extends even unto folly. The words of the Apostle remain eternally true, "Jesus Christ, yesterday, and today; and the same forever." (*Heb.* 13:8).

A Personal Love

Besides the many marvelous proofs of His love for all mankind, Jesus gives numberless proofs of a **personal** love for each one of us. Does He not come personally into our hearts to receive a love and gratitude which only we can give Him? Does He not come to **each one** of His children, to speak to him, to embrace him, to enrich him with the treasures of His grace? His visit is always so kind, so loving. No matter how many receive Him, He still gives Himself wholly and entirely to **each one.** Each one receives Him entirely, without disadvantage to others, as St. Thomas says so beautifully in the hymn *Lauda Sion:* "Whether one or thousands eat, All receive the self-same meat, Nor the less for others leave."

On the altar He sacrifices Himself not

only on behalf of all mankind, but for each soul in particular. And if the church is filled with worshippers, each one can still pray to Jesus, speak to Him heart to heart, ask graces and personal favors of Him. He listens to each one personally as though that person were alone in the church, for He loves each one of us individually with an infinite, undying love. Access to Him is always possible; it matters not whether we come in the morning, at noon or at night. He is there for each one of us, whether we be great or lowly, rich or poor. His assistance is always at our disposal, in every necessity, spiritual and temporal. Ah, that our faith, our confidence, our fidelity were never wanting, and that in all our necessities we would seek help from the all-powerful, all-wise and all-loving Saviour who dwells in our Tabernacles!

The sacramental presence of Our Lord makes the Tabernacle a throne of grace, where He constantly gives audience to all who have petitions to present, and where we poor, blind, lame and leprous children of men may approach and cry out to Him: "Have mercy on us!" In our days, as of yore, He will produce in those who implore Him,

all the effects of grace and salvation which
went forth from Him during His earthly life.

O Jesus in the Most Blessed Sacrament,
have mercy on us!

All love, honor and glory
to the Eucharistic Heart of Jesus.

Chapter 5

The Center of Catholic Worship

THE Church understands what a treasure she possesses in this Sacrament; she understands what a precious inheritance her Divine Founder has left her in this sublime legacy; she knows how to esteem and to preserve this priceless jewel confided to her virginal hands. She acknowledges in this Sacrament her highest good, and makes It the center of her worship. In truth, the mystery of the Holy Eucharist forms the center of all her feasts, of her entire liturgy, of her whole life. Even those with only a rudimentary knowledge of the Church and her teachings know that all her liturgy and ceremonial surround the Blessed Sacrament. The cornerstone of our entire belief, the greatest treasure we have on earth and the hope of our reward in Heaven is centered in the consecrated Host which reposes on our altars and in our Tabernacles.

All the thoughts and desires of the Church proceed from the Holy Eucharist and revert thereto. It is her strength, her consolation, her joy, her glory. It is that great Sacrifice by which she offers a worthy homage to the Triune God, reconciles her children with Him, returns thanks, and implores grace and mercy. It is that powerful means by which she strengthens her children on the way of Christian perfection and encourages them continually to aspire to higher things. It is the light of her confessors, the purity of her virgins, the fortitude of her martyrs and the strength of her Apostles. It is for all her children the "Bread of Life," the Bread which came down from Heaven, containing in Itself all sweetness. It is, in a word, her ALL IN ALL.

Many and varied are the devotions practiced by the children of the holy Catholic Church. Some of these are practiced throughout all Christendom, in all parts of the world, in all countries and in all places, by persons of every age, of every rank and walk of life. Others, again, are more suitable for certain states or vocations, for certain ages or particular places. But the most universally practiced, the "queen of all devotions," is devotion to the Blessed Sacrament. It is the central devotion of the Church. All others group themselves around it as satellites, for others celebrate the mysteries of our holy Faith, but this is **God Himself.** It is the devotion of all races, of all lands, of all ages, of all classes, of all times.*

The Holy Eucharist is the very life of the Church, for it is not only the gift presented by Jesus, but the very living Jesus Himself. It is the triumph of the Most Holy Trinity. Yes, all the art and ceremonial, the liturgical wisdom and the rubrical majesty of the Church are grouped around the Blessed Sacrament. This one devotion unites and comprehends all the others.

The Most Sublime Devotion

The Saints in Heaven deserve our veneration because of their dignity and exalted state; they deserve to be imitated in their

---

*By "devotion to the Blessed Sacrament" we are not referring to the formal worship which we render to God by the Holy Sacrifice of the Mass or by the reception of Holy Communion, but rather the homage and love with which we surround Our Lord on our altars in His sacramental state outside of Holy Mass.

virtues and good deeds. We ask their intercession on account of their power with God. Devotion to the Saints is encouraged by the Church and practiced by all her children. We all have our favorites among that glorious company of God's friends, to whom we confide our difficulties and whom we honor with special marks of affection. But no saint—not even the Blessed Virgin Mary, the Queen of Saints—can compare in dignity, holiness, goodness and power with our Divine Lord and Saviour, **Jesus Christ.** For in Jesus, the Saint of saints, all perfections extend to the infinite. Clearly, then, devotion to Jesus in the Holy Eucharist is the most sublime of all devotions and renders the greatest honor and glory to God. In other devotions we honor God's creatures, but in the Blessed Sacrament we honor **the Creator Himself.**

Oh, rapturous thought! I kneel at the foot of the altar. A few steps away is **my Saviour,** really, truly and substantially present. There, in the Sacred Host, my Creator, the Lord of the universe, is enthroned. There in the Tabernacle dwells the Founder and Protector of His Church—my God, whom I shall once behold in untold glory and in whom even here below I find my joy and bliss. There He abides with the same **Precious Blood** which He shed for my salvation, with that same blessed **Soul** which is the most marvelous of God's works of creation, with that same Deified **Heart** which contains all the treasures of the Godhead. And it is to Him that I offer adoration, praise and thanksgiving when I worship the Blessed Sacrament.

Union of All Devotions

The excellence of devotion to the Most Holy Eucharist is evident also from the way in which it wonderfully unites and comprises every other devotion.

The **Saints** can be honored in no more perfect manner than by offering the Holy Sacrifice of the Mass in their honor. Every altar on which the Eucharistic Sacrifice is offered must enclose the relics of saints, and in every Holy Mass they are invoked and commemorated. The Angels, likewise, receive special mention in the prayers and in the Preface of the Mass, and no act of veneration redounds so greatly to their glory as the Eucharistic Sacrifice. The **Blessed**

Virgin Mary, too, shares in a most intimate manner in the honor rendered to God through Eucharistic devotion, as is shown by the manner in which the Church combines her veneration with the worship of her Divine Son on the altar. Indeed, the sacred Body of Christ in the Holy Eucharist is Flesh of her flesh and Blood of her blood, so that she has been fittingly accorded the title of "Our Lady of the Blessed Sacrament."

The adoration which we pay to the Holy Eucharist redounds also in a special manner to the honor and glory of the **Triune God.** For, as the Father, the Son and the Holy Ghost are substantially and indissolubly united with one another, so the Father and the Holy Ghost, in virtue of this wonderful union, are present upon the altar with the Son of God. And therefore in rendering worship to Jesus in the Blessed Sacrament, we worship at one and the same time the other two Persons of the Blessed Trinity.

Devotion to the Blessed Sacrament is also the most excellent manner of glorifying the **Sacred Heart** of Jesus, His **Precious Blood,** His **Holy Wounds,** and all the members of His Sacred Humanity to which we direct our loving devotion.

Renewal of All the Mysteries
of the Redemption

In every Holy Mass, the incomprehensible mystery of the Incarnation is mystically renewed when the priest pronounces the words of Consecration. In His sacramental state He continues that life of helplessness and imprisonment which He lived in the bosom of His virginal Mother. In Holy Mass He renews in a mysterious manner the mystery of His sacred birth. His hidden life at Bethlehem, Egypt and Nazareth finds its counterpart in His hidden life in the Tabernacle. How beautifully, also, is His public life of ministry reproduced in the Blessed Sacrament! What silent words, what works of mercy, what miracles of grace are issuing from Him all day long in the darkness of the Tabernacle!

The Passion and death of Christ are also renewed on the altar, for the Sacrifice of the Mass is the unbloody renewal of the Sacrifice of Calvary itself. On the altar our Saviour offers Himself for the sins of the world just as efficaciously as He once offered Himself on the Cross.

The mystery of the Resurrection is

renewed in the Blessed Sacrament, for here Jesus is present with that transfigured Body which came forth from the tomb on Easter morning, glorious and immortal, no longer capable of suffering or death. And finally, His admirable Ascension is also renewed, for in the Holy Eucharist Jesus lives the life of glory which He lives at the right hand of His Father in Heaven.

Words of Pope Leo XIII

On the eve of Corpus Christi, 1902, Pope Leo XIII issued an encyclical concerning the Most Holy Eucharist in which he spoke of this Sacrament as the center of the Christian life, in which all practices of devotion have their focus and their final end. He called the Eucharist "the Divine gift of Redemption," "the most efficacious means for overcoming the evils of the times." Let us quote a few sentences from this inspiring encyclical:

> All life and all good comes to us through Jesus Christ . . . The fountain and origin of all this is chiefly the Holy Eucharist; It even makes us partakers of

the Divine nature. . . . The Holy Eucharist gives growth in virtue; It is the pledge of glory for body and soul. . . . The Holy Eucharist gives an increase of love—the love of God and the love of our neighbor. . . .

But, indeed, a Sacrament so great and so rich in all manner of blessings can never be extolled as It deserves by human eloquence, nor adequately venerated by the worship of man. This Sacrament, whether as the theme of devout meditation, or as the object of public adoration, or, best of all, as a food to be received in the utmost purity of conscience, is to be regarded as the center toward which the spiritual life of a Christian in all its ambit gravitates; for all other forms of devotion, whatsoever they may be, lead up to It, and in It find their completion. In this Mystery, more than in any other, that gracious promise of Christ is realized and finds its daily fulfillment: "Come to Me, all you that labor and are burdened, and I will refresh you." (*Matt.* 11:28).

Further the Encyclical reads:

> History bears witness that the virtues of Christian life have flourished best wherever and whenever the frequent reception of the Eucharist has most prevailed. On the other hand it is no less certain that in days when men have ceased to care for this Heavenly Bread, and have lost their relish for It, the practice of the Christian religion has gradually lost its force and vigor. It has always been the desire of the Church that at every Holy Mass the faithful should partake of this Divine Banquet.

Truly, devotion to the Most Holy Sacrament should hold the first place among all our devotions. It deserves the first place in the heart and in the life of every Catholic. If hitherto we have been cold and wanting in love, let us promise Jesus that it shall be different henceforth. Yes, let each one of us say: "I will love my Lord Jesus Christ in the Blessed Sacrament with my whole heart. I will think of Him, visit Him often, and in particular I will assist at Holy Mass frequently and receive Him often in Holy Communion."

Chapter 6

Proper Homage to the Blessed Sacrament

A Homage of Faith

THE Holy Eucharist calls for the exercise of a firm and lively faith. By professing our faith in the Real Presence we offer to God the most precious of our natural gifts—our understanding. Our senses perceive nothing on the altar to support our faith. In the crib and on the Cross, our Saviour was humiliated, yet there was some satisfaction for the senses. His Divinity was hidden, it is true, but His Humanity was visible. On the altar, however, His Sacred Humanity is concealed as completely as is His Divinity. In the crib and on the Cross, the Incarnate Son of God had witnesses to take the place, we may say, of His heavenly court. The Angels who announced His birth to the shepherds, the wonderful star that led the Magi to the crib, the sun that was darkened at His crucifixion, the trembling earth, the dead who came forth from their graves—all these were as so many witnesses to His Divinity. But we find nothing of this on the altar. Here the testimony of God is the sole support of our faith; here we must believe without the aid of our exterior senses.

A Homage of Love

Devotion to the Holy Eucharist is also a most worthy homage of love. Jesus subjected Himself to untold humiliations and insults in order to become our Brother, our Food, our Sacrifice. Can we consider this utter abasement of our Saviour without feeling moved to make Him a return of love?

Who can form an idea of how many impulses of glowing zeal the Holy Eucharist has excited in the hearts of Christians of all ages, of the magnanimous resolutions which It has inspired, the holy deeds which It has produced! Does it not seem, and fittingly so, that the creature in this devotedness to his hidden God desires to vie with the Creator Himself?

Bodily Homage

Great honor and glory are given to God also by the bodily homage we render to Him, in assuming the various postures and observing the various rites and ceremonies which the Church prescribes in her devotions. Bodily worship holds a considerable place not only in the corporate life of the Church, but in the life of each one of its members. It is a mode of prayer Divinely ordered, befitting the complex nature of man; for, being composed of flesh and spirit, of soul and body, man is bound in strict justice to approach God with his **whole being,** and to worship the Divine Majesty at once with his body of flesh and with his spiritual soul. The body likewise is a creation, a most wonderful creation of the Almighty, and it is fitting that it, too, should render its meed of homage to the Creator. In fact, it is compelled thereto by the very laws of nature, since we can perform no single act of the mind without some participation of our bodily organs. Our Lord Himself and His Blessed Mother rendered a most sublime bodily worship to the Triune God.

It should be our greatest care, therefore,

to render a fitting bodily worship by reverence and decorum in our deportment in the presence of the Blessed Sacrament and by modesty in our dress. Deplorable indeed is the laxity in this regard which modern fashions have introduced. Too often even supposedly fervent Catholics enter the house of God in a garb more suited to an athletic field or a pleasure resort, and their behavior is in accord with their dress. Alas, how the Heart of Jesus must bleed at this lack of consideration for His august Presence and the scandal given to others, perhaps even those not of our Faith! We would not think of entering thus into the presence of the great ones of this world, nor would we wish to make ourselves guilty of any breach of etiquette, for fear of becoming an object of contempt or ridicule. Let us, then, bear always in mind that **when we enter the church we are in the presence of God Himself**—the King of kings and Lord of lords—and strive to give outward expression to our faith by a becoming modesty in our dress and demeanor.

We should strive, too, to make our homage a **conscious** act of worship, avoiding all carelessness and thoughtlessness in performing the customary acts of reverence, such as genuflecting, making the Sign of the Cross, folding our hands and kneeling during the Divine services. Only then will our worship be worthy of our Divine Lord in the Blessed Sacrament and in keeping with our sublime dignity of children of God and members of the Mystical Body of Jesus Christ.

Perpetual Adoration— A Sublime Vocation

It has been truly said that **never is man greater than when he kneels in adoration before his God veiled in the Holy Eucharist.** How sublime, then, is the vocation of the perpetual adorer who is privileged to kneel so often in the presence of the Blessed Sacrament! At this sacred post of duty, the adorer renders a solemn homage of adoration, thanksgiving, reparation and petition in the name of the Church, and becomes the channel of immense treasures of grace which God pours out upon all mankind. What an unheard-of dignity!

The perpetual adoration of the Most Blessed Sacrament is an angelic service, an act of sublime faith and ardent love, a signal act of reparation to the Divine Heart of Jesus, a support for the Church Militant, a cause of special delight for the Church Triumphant and a source of indescribable relief for the members of the Church Suffering in Purgatory. It is not surprising, therefore, that the grace of an attraction toward the Holy Eucharist is considered one of the greatest graces God can bestow upon a soul. In His Divine goodness He gives this attraction to many souls, yet there are many who lack the generosity of heart to respond to the Divine call. Alas, what a loss to themselves and to the Church of God! Happy, indeed, are they who respond to the call of grace with a generous heart and who in a life of devoted service of the Blessed Sacrament enjoy even here below a foretaste of the peace and joy of Heaven.

Chapter 7

The Hope and Salvation of Our Times

THE Popes of modern times have been unanimous in proclaiming the Holy Eucharist to be the hope and salvation of the world in our evil and dangerous era. By word and example they have striven to bind the faithful more closely to their Eucharistic Lord, that they may draw from Him the light and strength they need in their temptations, anxieties and difficulties.

Pope Leo XIII, whose great sanctity of life and brilliant intellectual gifts made him one of the most illustrious of the Popes who have graced the Chair of Peter, once addressed these prophetic words to a famous Italian preacher: "Our Lord came to the aid of each great tribulation with a special devotion. The present and future tribulations of the Church and of nations are greater than at any other period, and this persecution is more dangerous than those of previous times. Hence, **the devotion which God sends to the succor of His Church and of the nations at the present time is the devotion to the Most Holy Eucharist.** It is the highest of all devotions. Preach this ever and always. Holy Communion must again be received frequently, yea, daily; the practices of the first Christian centuries must again be adopted."

His saintly successor, Pope St. Pius X, realizing likewise that the faithful were facing very critical times, strongly urged the reception of Holy Communion frequently and, if possible, daily, and decreed that even little children should be nourished with the Bread of Life as soon as they attained the use of reason. The zeal of this holy Pontiff in fostering love for the Blessed Sacrament has been immortalized in the endearing title of the "Pope of the Eucharist," which has been fittingly applied to him.

Pope Benedict XV likewise venerated the Holy Eucharist with glowing love, and, like his predecessors, regarded devotion to the Blessed Sacrament as the one great means of saving the world from the grave dangers which threatened its destruction. In an audience given to the religious of the Blessed Sacrament in September, 1914, he said: "You must propagate veneration of the Most Blessed Sacrament with all your might, for the devotion to the Holy Eucharist is the queen of all devotions." In December, 1914, he addressed a brief to the congress of "Priests of Perpetual Adoration" in Canada, in which he said:

> Nothing is nearer to Our heart than that devotion to the Holy Eucharist grow from day to day throughout the world. We earnestly desire that priests dedicate themselves to the Blessed Sacrament in such a manner that by It they become inflamed with glowing ardor, and, as it were, emit everywhere the sparks of Divine love.

Pope Pius XI, throughout his long and arduous pontificate, desired most earnestly that the fire of love for the Real Presence of Christ in the Holy Eucharist might be more and more kindled in the hearts of men, and that the Most Blessed Sacrament should be recognized as the bond of peace and reconciliation for Christian nations.

"The Divine Eucharist," he declared,

> forms the principal substance of the
> Christian's life; It is the inexhaustible
> source of consolations and supernatural
> comforts which soothes the sorrows and
> sufferings of poor mankind better than
> any human remedy. Jesus in the Holy
> Eucharist is the clement and peaceful
> King who still lives amongst us under
> the Sacramental veils.

Before his accession to the papacy, while librarian in Milan, he founded a congregation of nuns whose duty it was to render solemn adoration to the Most Blessed Sacrament and to induce the faithful to come to adore the Most Holy Eucharist exposed.

Pope Pius XII likewise found in the Blessed Sacrament his one great source of strength and support in bearing the onerous burdens of the papacy, which were made increasingly burdensome by the great upheaval of the world at that time. Again and again the Holy Father pointed out that the evils of the times were due to the abandonment of Christ by peoples and nations and urged the pastors of His flock to gather the faithful around the altars, to offer the Eucharistic Sacrifice and to implore of our Divine Saviour the restoration of peace and order to the disrupted world.

In an address to a group of pilgrims, Pope Pius said, regarding those who have strayed far from God and His Church:

> May they recognize this, and understand that Christ—notwithstanding the defections and denials and outrages—still and always remains near them, with extended arms and open Heart, ready to say to them, "Peace be with you," if they themselves, with a sincere and trusting impetus, will fall at His feet with that cry of love, "My Lord and my God!"

In the first encyclical letter issued by him after his accession to the papal throne, for the Feast of Christ the King in 1939, the Holy Father wrote, in part:

> In the midst of this world, which today presents such a sharp contrast to "the Peace of Christ in the Reign of Christ,"* the Church and her faithful are

---

*This was the motto of Pope Pius XI.

in times and in years of trial such as have rarely been known in her history of struggle and suffering. But in such times especially, he who remains firm in his faith and strong at heart knows that Christ the King is never so near as in the hour of trial, which is the hour for fidelity . . . Pray, then, venerable brethren, pray without ceasing; pray especially when **you offer the Divine Sacrifice of Love.** Do you, too, pray, whose courageous profession of Faith entails today, hard, painful, and not rarely heroic sacrifices; pray, you suffering and agonizing members of the Church, when **Jesus comes to console and to heal your pains . . .** that He in His mercy may shorten the days of trial . . . And you, white legions of children, who are so loved and dear to Jesus, **when you receive in Holy Communion the Bread of Life,** raise up your simple and innocent prayers and unite them with those of the Universal Church . . .

Let us take courage then in the thought that although we are living in exceedingly dangerous and turbulent times, we are also living in the **age of the Eucharist**, and that on our altars and in our Tabernacles the Lord of hosts dwells in all the omnipotence of His Divinity and the loving kindness of His Sacred Humanity, to comfort and sustain those who place their trust in Him. In His own good time, He will dispel the clouds of war and restore peace to the world, for He alone is "the Way, the Truth and the Life," not only of individual souls but also of nations.

Chapter 8

God So Near

ONE thought especially ought to incite us to devotion to the Most Blessed Sacrament, namely the **nearness of God, His abiding with us.** Mindful of His promise: "Behold, I am with you all days, even to the consummation of the world" (*Matt.* 28:20), our God finds His delight to dwell among us, His lowly creatures. But where does He dwell? We all know. We need but direct our footsteps to the church, we need but raise our eyes to the altar, to the tabernacle. There is the true "dwelling of God with men" (*Apoc.* 21:3); there is the "holy city," the "New Jerusalem," which St. John beheld in rapture, beautifully adorned as a bride descending from Heaven. Truly, "Terrible is this place; this is no other but the house of God, and the gate of heaven." (*Gen.* 28:17).

God's nearness to us is designated by Hettinger, a famous writer, as **the deepest essence of all religion.**

> God far from man, man far from God—this is the essence of irreligion in doctrine and life, in whatever forms they may appear. Modern paganism—what is it but the loud, powerful call of humanity for their God whom they have lost, who has concealed Himself behind the curtain of His Creation.

Lavater, a Protestant clergyman and poet, once said: "Could I believe that Christ is present in the Blessed Sacrament, I would ever remain on my knees in adoration."

Prince Hohenlohe expresses himself similarly in his memoirs:

> Had I the faith of the Crusaders, and were I convinced that Christ is present upon the altar in the monstrance, I could never more leave the church, but would lie prostrate before the Blessed Sacrament all day long, and would become a monk of the strictest observance.

A friend of St. John of Avila once said to

him: "If Jerusalem were in the hands of the Christians and I could take up my abode there, oh, how happy would I be in the grotto of Bethlehem, in the Cenacle (the room of the Last Supper), on Mount Calvary and at the Holy Sepulchre."

"What?" replied the holy man, briefly and to the point, "have we not the Blessed Sacrament here with us?" In other words, he wished to say: "He for whose sake you so highly esteem those holy places is here **in Person** truly and substantially present under the Sacramental veils."

"Thou art nigh unto us, O Lord," exclaimed the royal psalmist; and Moses called the people of Israel happy because no other nation "hath gods so nigh them, as our God." (*Deut.* 4:7). And yet, in the Old Law God manifested His special presence only in the Jewish tabernacle, and later in the Temple of Jerusalem; that is, in **one** place only. The Israelites who wished to go to their God had to go to that particular place, which for most of them entailed a long and tedious journey.

How near, on the other hand, is God to **us.** To us, far more than to the Israelites, may be applied the words of David and

Moses. God abides with us in thousands of churches. No one needs to travel far to visit Him. For us, God is truly **Emmanuel**—that is, **God with us.** And yet, alas, how seldom we visit this God of Love, who abases Himself to the extent of assuming the form of an insignificant wafer of bread in order to be able to remain ever with us and still not dazzle us by His splendor and majesty. Love keeps our Lord and God imprisoned, as it were, and we are so indifferent as to pass the church without stopping in to greet Him, without even thinking of Him. To many of us, perhaps, may be applied the reproachful words of St. John the Baptist to the Jews, "There hath stood one in the midst of you, whom you know not." (*John* 1:26).

Let us in the future overcome this coldness; let us take delight in visiting and adoring our dear Lord, daily, if possible. If, during life, we have loved Jesus above everything and have often visited and adored Him in our churches, what trust and confidence will fill our hearts when on our deathbed we receive Him in Holy Viaticum and prepare to meet Him as our merciful Judge.

Chapter 9

Heaven upon Earth

ALL men yearn for happiness, and all strive by every means in their power to obtain it; they think, dream and speak of happiness. Take away this longing, this striving from the human heart, and it will languish and sink into sadness and despair. Most people, however, have only their *temporal* happiness in view. They would have unclouded joy all the days of their life. *Heaven upon earth* is what they desire, and this is the end and aim of all their aspirations.

Such happiness as that desired by worldly-minded people is not to be found here on earth. This earth will ever remain a valley of tears, a place where care and sorrow, pain and sickness, mourning and death will ever dwell. True Christians, therefore, do not seek their Heaven upon earth in perishable things, but, as St. Paul admonishes, they "seek the things that are above, where Christ is sitting at the right hand of God." (*Col.* 3:1). They mind not the things of earth, but have their hearts set on the imperishable treasures of eternity. They bear all toil and fatigue for the love of God; they suffer and pray with eyes directed to their heavenly home. They know that crosses and trials borne in patience, in union with their suffering Redeemer, will infallibly lead them to the eternally beautiful Heaven beyond; they know that he who wishes to have an earthly heaven in this world must fear to lose the true, eternal Heaven which is the home of God. And such God-loving souls find a little heaven in the sanctuary of their own heart, where in loving union with God they enjoy a peace and happiness which the world can neither give nor take away from them.

The Heaven of the Tabernacle

And yet, there *is* a true heaven here upon earth, a heaven so genuine, so beautiful, so grace-abounding, that the human heart finds in it a true foretaste of the joys of Paradise. This heaven is the **Eucharistic Tabernacle,** where our God dwells with us in the Blessed Sacrament. Before the Tabernacle all our labors are lightened and sweetened; there our heart is satiated with the Bread of Life. There we receive eternal, inexpressibly precious graces and gifts.

Once when the Venerable Balthasar Alvarez, the confessor of St. Teresa, knelt before the Tabernacle, Jesus appeared to him in the form of a child, His little hands filled to overflowing with pearls and diamonds—so many, that He could scarcely hold them. Looking at Balthasar with a sorrowful expression, the Divine Child said to him with touching pathos: *If only someone would take them from Me!*

Every Catholic should be impressed with joyful amazement and deepest gratitude at sight of the condescension which God manifests in the Holy Eucharist, and should, without intermission, praise this celestial gift, this Manna from Heaven. Whoever regards this wonderful gift of God with indifference forgets that in the Tabernacle the same God is present who conversed with our first parents in Paradise and spoke to Moses from the burning bush; that in the

Tabernacle dwells the same God who once in human form walked upon earth and brought to mankind the glad tidings of salvation; who comforted the sorrowing, healed the sick and raised the dead to life. He forgets that the white Host conceals the God who once lay as a tiny Infant in the crib, and that from the altar the same Divine eye looks upon him whose dying gaze was bent upon the Blessed Mother and the beloved disciple at the foot of the Cross.

Through the Blessed Sacrament earth is made, in very deed, a vestibule of Heaven. The supreme happiness of Heaven consists in possessing God. The Blessed in Heaven behold God face to face; they know Him, they love Him and are most intimately united with Him. According to the Prophet Ezechiel, the name of the new holy city of Heaven and the name of the Church on earth shall be: **The Lord is there!** (*Ezech.* 48:35). In the same sense St. John writes: "Behold the tabernacle of God with men, and **he will dwell with them.** And they shall be His people and God Himself with them shall be their God." (*Apoc.* 21:3).

It would, indeed, be something great if a seraph or a saint were to dwell among us in the form of bread; but how we should marvel at the love of **the eternal God who dwells among us in so condescending a manner!** God revealed His presence in the Ark of the Covenant by listening to the prayers of the Jews and granting them many graces and favors, but He did not reveal Himself with that real and personal presence which He accords us in the Blessed Sacrament. Oh, let us appreciate this unspeakable gift!

On the first Sunday of Lent in the year 1585, St. Teresa appeared to Father Jerome Gratian and said to him:

> We in Heaven and you on earth must be alike in purity and love; we in perfect enjoyment, and you in suffering. What we in Heaven do before the Divine Reality, that you on earth must do before the Blessed Sacrament. Announce this to all my daughters.

Blessed Crescentia of Kaufbeuren often said: "Two things constitute my Heaven on earth: **The holy Will of God and the Most Blessed Sacrament.**" Heaven is a state of perfect and eternal happiness, the spiritual possession of God, beholding Him face to face in the Beatific Vision and loving Him to the utmost of the creature's powers in communion with the Blessed Virgin Mary, the Angels and the Saints. In the Blessed Sacrament we come closest to the supreme bliss of Heaven for we possess the same God who is the joy of the Blessed, in whose presence the Angels veil their faces and sing their **Sanctus, sanctus, sanctus!**—"Holy, holy, holy!"—the God whom they reverently surround in every Tabernacle where He is present. Yes, we possess God and can even receive into our very being in Holy Communion Him who is the "Bread of Angels," the "Manna from Heaven," who becomes, as St. Thomas writes in the *Lauda Sion,* "the Food of pilgrims striving for Heaven."

The Delight of the Saints

Oh, what a heaven the Saints found on earth in their ardent devotion to the Most Blessed Sacrament! They indeed experienced that to none is Jesus so lavish of His sensible graces as to those who have a fervent devotion to the Blessed Sacrament. What sighs of love, what sweet tears and raptures, what floods of delight and consolation overwhelmed their souls when they celebrated or approached the Sacred Mysteries! Many Saints received Holy Communion from the hands of Angels; others lived for years without food other than the Holy Eucharist.

In truth, **there is no place where our Divine Saviour is more generous than upon the altar,** where He makes the sweetness of His presence and of His gifts more susceptible, for it is His delight to be with the children of men. Oh, let us, too, foster a tender devotion to the Holy Eucharist; let us, too, seek this "Heaven on earth," in which the Saints found such supreme delight.

Prayers

Prayer to Jesus in the Blessed Sacrament

O AMIABLE JESUS, Who hast given us, in the adorable Eucharist, so convincing a proof of Thine infinite love, permit us to thank Thee, in the name of all Thy creatures, for the many blessings contained in this one precious gift. We adore Thee, O hidden Deity, and most ardently wish we could offer Thee such love as would atone for our own offenses and for those committed by all mankind against this most adorable Mystery of Love.

We ask pardon, O Lord, for the transgressions we have committed against Thee. We are truly sorry for having offended Thee, because Thou art infinitely good. A contrite and humble heart Thou wilt not despise. We desire to love Thee more and more, and we beseech Thee for the grace of perseverance. Convinced that our confidence in Thee cannot be too great, we come now to implore of Thee, by that infinite love which induced Thee to institute this adorable Sacrament, and by all the graces which have ever flowed from this source of every blessing, to grant us the favor we now implore.

We firmly purpose to become more fervent and more devoted adorers of this Sacrament of Love, and to take Thy Eucharistic life for the rule and model of our own. Give us grace to honor Thy silence on our altars, by the spirit of recollection and prayer; Thy poverty, obedience and adorable sanctity, by detachment from all things, renunciation of self-will and horror of sin. Above all, we beseech Thee, O Living Bread of eternal life, to remove all obstacles to our receiving Thee more fruitfully and worthily; and grant to us so tender a devotion to this amiable Mystery that our hearts and thoughts may ever be turned to Thee, present on our altars, and that every action of our lives may be directed to the perfect accomplishment of Thy holy Will. Amen.

Prayer for Faith in the Real Presence

WE COME to Thee, dear Lord, like the Apostles, saying: *Increase our faith.* Give us a strong and lively faith in the Real Presence. Give us the splendid faith of the centurion which drew from Thee such praise. Give us the faith of the beloved disciple to recognize Thee and say: *It is the Lord.* Give us the faith of Peter to confess: *Thou art Christ, the Son of the Living God.* Give us the faith of Magdalen to fall at Thy feet, crying: *Rabboni, Master!*

Give us the faith of all Thy Saints to whom the Blessed Sacrament was Heaven begun on earth. In every Communion and at every visit, increase our faith and love, our humility and reverence, and all good things will come to us. Dearest Lord, *increase our faith!*

I adore Thee, O most sacred
Eucharistic Heart of Jesus!

 **TAN·BOOKS**

TAN Books was founded in 1967 to preserve the spiritual, intellectual and liturgical traditions of the Catholic Church. At a critical moment in history TAN kept alive the great classics of the Faith and drew many to the Church. In 2008 TAN was acquired by Saint Benedict Press. Today TAN continues its mission to a new generation of readers.

From its earliest days TAN has published a range of booklets that teach and defend the Faith. Through partnerships with organizations, apostolates, and mission-minded individuals, well over 10 million TAN booklets have been distributed.

More recently, TAN has expanded its publishing with the launch of Catholic calendars and daily planners—as well as Bibles, fiction, and multimedia products through its sister imprints Catholic Courses (catholiccourses.com) and Saint Benedict Press (saintbenedictpress.com).

Today TAN publishes over 500 titles in the areas of theology, prayer, devotions, doctrine, Church history, and the lives of the saints. TAN books are published in multiple languages and found throughout the world in schools, parishes, bookstores and homes.

For a free catalog, visit us online at
TANBooks.com

Or call us toll-free at
(800) 437-5876